I0435262

BATS

Sandie Lee Books

Bats

There are over 1,200 different bat species on the planet today. In fact, the bat makes up one quarter of all the species of animals. That is a lot of bats! The bat species is broken into two different categories; Megachiroptera (Megabats or large) and Microchiroptera (Microbats or small). People either love them or hate them, but one thing is for sure, the bat is truly fascinating. Let's explore the world of the bat to see what other facts we can dig up.

Where in the World?

Did you know bats are found almost everywhere on Earth? The bat can be anywhere in the world, except the polar regions and extreme desert regions. Fruit bats can be found in the tropical rainforests, where some smaller bats can be found in attics, church steeples, barns and other places.

The Body of a Bat

Did you know bats can range in size from very small to very large?   Megabats are the largest. Their wingspan can reach 5.6 feet in length. Microbats are smaller and can be as tiny as a bumblebee. The body of the bat is covered with fur and it has short legs with five toes on each foot.

The Bat's Wings

Did you know the bat's wings are really part of its arm and hands? The wing of the bat is made up of two thin layers of skin. The skin is stretched over its arms and "fingers." Like us, the bat has 4 fingers and a thumb. The skin on the wing runs all along its body and partway down its legs.

The Bat's Senses

Did you know bats are not really blind? Bats can see well in the daytime, but their eyesight is reduced at night. Bats have excellent hearing. Some species of bats have huge ears compared to the rest of their head. Fruit bats use their sense of smell to locate ripe fruit.

The Wintertime Bat

Did you know some bats migrate and others hibernate during the cold winter months? Some species of the bat will journey many miles to warmer climates before winter. This is called, migrating. Other bats will find a cozy cave or other sheltered places to sleep away the winter. This is called, hibernation.

What a Bat Eats

Did you know the bat can eat many different types of foods, even blood?   Depending on the species, bats will hunt and eat insects, nectar, fruit, pollen, frogs, fish and blood. The Vampire bat will suck some blood from live mammals such as cattle.   Others can eat thousands of flying insects in one night.

The Bat's Special Ability

Did you know the bat uses echolocation to hunt for food at night? This is similar to us shouting and hearing an echo. The bat will make a high-pitched sound. This sound is sent out. When it bounces off of an object, the sound returns to the bat's ears. In this way, the bat can tell where objects are and the distance away it is located.

Bats as Prey

Did you know the bat can be hunted as food? Some large birds and animals will hunt bats. Raccoons, opossums, owls and pythons will catch and eat a bat. Humans have also been known to hunt this animal. Bats can be considered a nuisance when in people's homes, so they may be exterminated.

Bat Talk

Did you know the bat makes sounds? A big part of echolocation is based on sound. Bats can make high-pitched noises that humans cannot hear. This is how they hunt. Other sounds a bat will make are squeaks or clicking noises. Some male bats will sing, display their wings and stand the hair up on their heads to attract a mate.

Mother Bat

Did you know the mother bat only gives birth to one baby at a time? Depending on the species, female bats can carry their young from 40 days to 6 months. The mother bat still has to fly and search for food when she is pregnant. This can be a difficult task.

Baby Bats

Did you know baby bats are called, pups? A baby bat is born without fur. It is blind and its wings are not developed. It will nurse milk from its mother for several weeks. The baby bat clings to its mother's belly for warmth and protection. A baby bat can be raised with many other baby bats.

Life of a Bat

Did you know some bats can live a very long time? Depending on the species, a bat can live to be from 20 to 40 years-old. Bats play an important role on Earth. They can eat thousands of bugs each night. Pollen-eating bats help plants to grow and blossom. Fruit eating bats spread the seeds of the fruit to grow new fruit trees.

The Spotted Bat

This species of bat is in the Microbat family. It can measure almost 5 inches in length. This animal has very large ears. The ears can each be 1.5 inches long. Its fur is black with 3 white spots on its back. It mainly eats moths and grasshoppers and can be found in Utah, Arizona, California, Colorado and British Columbia, Canada.

The Fruit Bat

This type of bat is considered a Megabat. It is also called, a Flying Fox, in some areas. This bat's face looks like a small fox. It has sharp teeth and a very long tongue - these help it eat the fruit. The largest breed of this bat can grow to be 3.5 pounds, with a wingspan of 5.6 feet.

Quiz

Question 1: How many different species of bats are there?

Answer 1: 1,200

Question 2: What are the two categories bats fall into?

Answer 2: Megabats and Microbats

Question 3: What does the bat have that is similar to humans?

Answer 3: Four fingers and a thumb

Question 4: What does the fruit bat use its excellent sense of smell for?

Answer 4: To locate ripe fruit

Question 5: When a bat sends out a call and it bounces back to it, what is this called?

Answer 5: Echolocation

Thank you for checking out another addition from Sandie Lee Books! Make sure to check out Amazon.com for many other great titles.

www.ingramcontent.com/pod-product-compliance
Lightning Source LLC
Chambersburg PA
CBHW050800290526
45792CB00008B/2265